LIVING THE LIFE *of* FAITH

LIVING THE LIFE *of* FAITH

Bishop C.H. Wright

BISHOP C.H. WRIGHT PUBLISHING

Printed in the United States of America

ISBN: 979-8-9992198-0-0 (paperback)
ISBN: 979-8-9992198-1-7 (ebook)

Unless otherwise noted, all scriptures are from the Holy Bible, King James Version

Dedication

To every believer who has chosen to walk by faith even when the way was unclear—this book is for you.

To those who've dared to believe when the odds were stacked, when hope felt distant, and when the promise seemed impossible—may this book be a reminder that faith still moves mountains.

To my spiritual sons and daughters, ministry partners, and fellow laborers in the Kingdom—you are proof that a God kind of faith still changes lives. Keep standing, keep believing, and never stop declaring the Word.

-Bishop Connie Wright

CONTENTS

PREFACE

Every generation faces its own battles—uncertainty, fear, delay, and doubt. But the one constant that transcends time, culture, and crisis is **faith in the living God—not just belief in His existence** but full persuasion in His Word, His character, and His power to do what He has promised. This book, *A God Kind of Faith*, was birthed out of divine revelation and lived experience—a journey through the Word and the walk of faith.

Too often, we settle for surviving when God has called us to **reign in life** (Romans 5:17). This book is not a theoretical exploration but a spiritual impartation. It is written to equip every believer, from the seasoned saint to the new convert, to walk in the authority and confidence that comes from trusting God without compromise.

You will find in these pages' biblical examples, modern insights, and Holy Spirit-led truths that are not only informative but **transformational**. You will learn the difference between natural faith and supernatural faith, how to speak the Word with authority, and how to live with bold expectancy no matter the challenge. This book was written with one purpose in mind: **to awaken and strengthen the kind of faith that moves mountains, opens doors, and ushers in the miraculous**.

It is my prayer that as you read, **your faith will not only be stirred—but stretched**, until you begin to see, speak, and live according to **God's perspective**, not your own. May this book serve as both a mirror and a compass—showing you where you are, and guiding you into all that God has destined for your life.

Let every page remind you: **you were created to live by faith—and not just any faith, but a God kind of faith.**

| 1 |

THE LAW OF FAITH I

"Jesus lived according to the Law of Faith." — Bishop C.H. Wright

Before time began, before man drew breath, before the first miracle or mistake of man, God established a law that would govern all interaction between heaven and earth- God created **"Heaven's Operating System"** —the Law of Faith. This law is not religious suggestion, nor a mystical abstraction. It is heaven's operating system. Everything God does in the earth—every breakthrough, every promise fulfilled, every miracle released—moves through the pipeline of faith. To ignore this law is to disconnect from divine flow. To understand it is to align with supernatural power. In this chapter, we uncover what it means to walk by faith—not as mere theology, but as the key that unlocks God's promises in our lives. The question is no longer "Does God want to bless me?" but "Am I operating in the law that gives Him access?"

The Voice of God Still Speaks

Can you hear Him? That still, small voice echoes through eternity: *"I have dealt to every man the measure of faith. Use it."* (Romans 12:3, KJV). This is not a suggestion. It is not a whisper of possibility. This is the voice of Almighty God thundering into your reality, awakening the very force that moves mountains, opens the heavens, and changes destinies. The voice that called light into being is calling **you** into a walk—a life—of supernatural power. This is not the faith of man. This is **the God kind of faith.**

Before the foundations of the world, God established a spiritual law—one that governs how heaven invades earth. That law is not driven by sight, emotion, or circumstance. It is rooted in divine authority, eternal truth, and kingdom manifestation. That law is **The Law of Faith**.

What Is the Law of Faith?

According to the apostle Paul, "...God hath dealt to every man the measure of faith" (Romans 12:3, KJV). The New Living Translation says it this way: "Because of the privilege and authority God has given me, I give each of you this warning: Don't think you are better than you really are. Be honest in your evaluation of yourselves, measuring yourselves by the faith God has given us" (Romans 12:3, NLT).

The **Law of Faith** is the spiritual principle that governs how divine promises become earthly realities. Just as the law of gravity governs the physical world, the Law of Faith governs the spiritual realm. Faith is not merely belief—it is a divine transaction. Faith reaches into the unseen and pulls the promises of God into the now.

Faith: Defined by God

Faith is not wishing, hoping, or trying. According to Hebrews 11:1 (KJV), "Now faith is the substance of things hoped for, the evidence of things not seen." The Amplified Bible says, "Faith is the assurance (title deed, confirmation) of things hoped for (divinely guaranteed), and the evidence of things not seen [the conviction of their reality—faith comprehends as fact what cannot be experienced by the physical senses]."

Faith is **confidence in God's word** and **action based on that confidence**. It is the only currency heaven responds to. God does not respond to fear, need, or desperation. He responds to **faith**—His own Word returned to Him in belief and action.

Walking in the Law of Faith

To walk in the Law of Faith is to commit to a lifestyle that places full dependence on God's Word—regardless of sight, circumstances, or emotions. It is not a spiritual suggestion but a divine requirement. As stated in Habakkuk 2:3–4 (KJV), "For the vision is yet for an appointed time... but the just shall live by his faith." The Amplified Bible deepens our understanding, declaring, "But the [righteous] will live by his faith [in the true God]." This passage establishes a foundational principle in the kingdom of God: the just—the righteous, those in right standing with God—do not live by human logic, popular opinion, or religious routine. They live by faith.

This principle is not isolated to the Old Testament. It is powerfully echoed and affirmed across the New Testament in Romans 1:17, Galatians 3:11, and Hebrews 10:38. Paul writes in Romans 1:17 (KJV), "For therein is the righteousness of God revealed from faith to faith: as it is written, The just shall live by faith." Here, the apostle emphasizes that faith is not a one-time event but a progressive, ongoing journey—from "faith to faith." Galatians 3:11 makes it clear that justification before God does not come by keeping the law but by placing unwavering trust in His Word: "But that no man is justified by the law in the sight of God, it is evident: for, The just shall live by faith" (KJV). Hebrews 10:38 issues a sobering warning: "Now the just shall live by faith: but if any man draw back, my soul shall have no pleasure in him" (KJV). In other words, retreating into doubt, fear, or self-reliance not only displeases God but disconnects us from His promises. Faith is not optional; it is the spiritual atmosphere in which the believer must live, move, and have their being.

Living by faith requires more than mental agreement or emotional agreement, it is a deliberate daily decision. It is not the spiritual equivalent of an emergency parachute used only in crisis. Faith is the oxygen of the Spirit-filled life. Just as the body cannot function without breath, the spirit cannot thrive without faith. When believers walk in the Law of Faith, they make decisions based not on what they see, but on what God has said. They endure hardship, not because it is easy, but because they believe that God is faithful to His promises. Walking by faith means stepping into unknown territory, trusting that even when the path is unclear, God's Word is a lamp to our feet and a light to our path (Psalm 119:105, KJV).

This kind of walk is neither passive nor weak. It is bold, intentional, and rooted in a kingdom mindset. It trusts God with provision when there's lack, with healing when the report says otherwise, with peace when everything around screams chaos. It is the same kind of faith Abraham walked in when he left everything familiar to pursue a promise he had not yet seen. It is the same faith that allowed Moses to confront Pharaoh, David to face Goliath, and the early church to preach under persecution. Today, that same faith must govern our lives.

When we walk in the Law of Faith, we are not simply adhering to a religious principle—we are aligning ourselves with heaven's legal system. Faith is the kingdom's currency, and living by it grants us access to divine provision, protection, and purpose. It is the lens through which we see every situation differently, not as victims of circumstance but as victors through Christ Jesus. Walking in faith means we remain unmoved by what surrounds us because we are anchored in what God has spoken. His Word becomes our compass, His voice our command,

and His promise is our proof. So then, the just must do more than believe—they must live. Live with unwavering confidence. Live with unshakable trust. Live fully persuaded that what God has promised, He is well able to perform (Romans 4:21, KJV). This is what it means to walk in the Law of Faith—and this walk is not for thc faint of heart, but for the fully surrendered.

Crossing the Line from Unbelief to Belief

There is a defining moment in every believer's life—a spiritual threshold—where we are called to cross the invisible yet powerful line between unbelief and belief. This shift is not just internal; it determines whether we walk in divine power or remain bound by earthly limitation. In Mark 9:17–28 (KJV), we find a desperate father whose son is tormented by a spirit that renders him mute and throws him into life-threatening convulsions. After the disciples fail to deliver the child, the father turns to Jesus as a last resort, crying out, "If thou canst do anything, have compassion on us, and help us." But Jesus' response is stunning: *"If thou canst believe, all things are possible to him that believeth"* (v. 23). In one sentence, Jesus shifts the weight of the miracle—not on His power—but on the man's faith. The issue was never whether Jesus could do it; the question was, could the man believe?

This encounter reveals a divine truth: heaven is activated by belief. The father's son wasn't healed until the man crossed that line from doubt to belief. He immediately cried out in tears, "Lord, I believe; help thou mine unbelief" (v. 24), acknowledging both his faith and his struggle. This honesty was enough. Jesus, moved by that raw, transitioning faith, commanded the spirit to leave, and the boy was healed. The breakthrough came not when the man pleaded—but when he chose to believe. This moment illustrates a critical principle: faith is the bridge between human need and divine intervention.

Jesus reinforces this truth again in Matthew 17:20 (KJV) when He tells His disciples, "If ye have faith as a grain of mustard seed... nothing shall be impossible unto you." The significance of the mustard seed lies not in its size but in its potential. A mustard seed begins small but grows into something substantial and immovable. Jesus did not say we need massive, flawless faith—just genuine faith, no matter how small. It is not the volume of faith that matters but its presence. A whisper of belief—when aligned with God's Word—can move the mountains of sickness, fear, addiction, or despair.

When we cross that threshold from unbelief to belief, everything changes. It is at that very point that fear loses its grip, doubt is silenced, and the supernatural begins to invade the natural. This is the moment where the impossible becomes possible. Faith, even in its infancy, signals to heaven that we are ready to receive. God doesn't wait for perfect conditions—He responds to belief in action. The father in Mark 9 had no theology degree. He had no perfect track record of faith. But in his brokenness, he made the decision to believe. And that decision opened the door to his son's deliverance.

The same is true for us today. We stand at the edge of miracles more often than we realize, but the key to stepping into them lies in our willingness to believe. Jesus is still asking the question: *"If you can believe, all things are possible."* The invitation is there. The question is not whether He will move; the question is whether we will believe.

Faith in the Storm: Trusting the Presence Over the Problem

One of the clearest illustrations of how faith is tested—and revealed—is found in Mark 4:37–40 (KJV), where Jesus' disciples encounter a violent storm while crossing the Sea of Galilee. The storm arose suddenly, as was common in that region, and the waves beat into the boat so fiercely that it began to fill with water. The disciples, many of whom were seasoned fishermen, panicked in fear for their lives. Meanwhile, Jesus lay asleep on a pillow in the rear of the boat, completely undisturbed by the chaos around Him. In desperation, the disciples woke Him, crying out, "Master, carest thou not that we perish?" (v. 38). Their question was not just a plea for help—it was a reflection of their internal doubt. Fear had drowned out their awareness of who was in the boat with them.

Jesus arose, rebuked the wind, and said to the sea, "Peace, be still." Instantly, the wind ceased, and there was a great calm. But His next words to the disciples were not words of comfort—they were words of correction: *"Why are ye so fearful? How is it that ye have no faith?"* (Mark 4:40, KJV). This question reveals that Jesus was not upset about the storm itself, but about their reaction to it. The issue was not the storm's intensity, but the disciples' failure to remember His identity. The presence of Jesus in the boat should have been more powerful to them than the presence of the storm outside of it.

This moment teaches us a crucial truth about the faith walk: faith is not the absence of storms; it is the assurance of who is with us in the storm. Faith is not proven when everything is calm, but when everything is chaotic, and we still choose to trust. Jesus expected His disciples to rest in the reality that His presence was their protection. If He said, "Let us pass over unto the other side" (v. 35), then nothing—not even a violent storm—could stop them from arriving. Faith, therefore, means holding onto His word more tightly than we hold onto our fear.

In today's terms, this is similar to facing job loss, a health crisis, relational conflict, or a sudden tragedy—and still believing that God is in control. Faith is the steady voice that says, "Peace" in the middle of the storm. It does not deny the existence of the storm, but it refuses to be ruled by it. It declares that the Word and presence of Jesus are greater than any wave that crashes against our life.

Many believers waver not because Jesus is absent, but because they forget that He is present—and that His presence is always more powerful than the problem. Jesus did not promise that storms would never come; He promised that He would never leave us (Hebrews 13:5). A faith walk, then, is not one of constant clarity or comfort. It is a walk of confidence in the face of contradiction. It is responding to chaos with conviction, not confusion.

So, when the winds rise and the waves swell, let the response of faith be louder than the voice of fear. Let your heart be anchored in the knowledge that Jesus is not only aware—He is in the boat with you, ready to speak peace. And when He speaks, even the winds obey (Mark 4:41). That is the authority we walk in when we choose faith over fear.

Faith Must Be Put to Work: The Power of Believing and Doing

True faith is never idle. It demands expression, action, and obedience. The epistle of James makes this principle abundantly clear: **faith without corresponding works is dead**. In **James 2:17 (KJV)**, Scripture says, "Even so faith, if it hath not works, is dead, being alone." This is not a mere philosophical observation—it is a sobering warning. Intellectual agreement with the truth is not enough; biblical faith is always **accompanied by movement**, decision, and demonstrated trust. James further reinforces this point in verses 20 and 26, declaring, "But wilt thou know, O vain man, that faith without works is dead?" (v. 20) and "For as the body without the spirit is dead, so faith without works is dead also" (v. 26). In other words, faith that is not followed by obedient action is **lifeless and ineffective**. It may look like faith, sound like faith, and even feel like faith—but if it does not produce fruit, it is **functionally dead**.

Perhaps one of the most powerful examples of faith in action is found in the life of **Abraham**, the father of faith. According to **Hebrews 11:17–19 (KJV)**, "By faith Abraham, when he was tried, offered up Isaac... accounting that God was able to raise him up, even from the dead." Abraham's willingness to sacrifice his promised son reveals a level of trust in God that went far beyond belief. He didn't just believe **in** God—he believed **God's Word**, even when it contradicted his natural understanding. God had promised that Isaac would be the son through whom Abraham's descendants would come (Genesis 21:12). Yet when commanded to offer him as a sacrifice, Abraham did not hesitate. Why? Because he was fully persuaded that if necessary, **God would raise Isaac from the dead** to fulfill His promise. This wasn't passive hope—it was **active faith**, rooted in the character of God and demonstrated through radical obedience.

This is the **Law of Faith in operation**—faith that believes, speaks, and acts. Abraham didn't merely say he trusted God; he climbed a mountain, built an altar, and raised a knife. His actions aligned perfectly with his belief. That is the essence of real faith: it compels us to act in accordance with what God has said, even when the outcome is uncertain, uncomfortable, or humanly impossible.

In today's world, this might look like launching a business when God says "go," even when resources are limited. It may mean forgiving someone when your emotions scream otherwise, or sowing a financial seed when your budget says no. Faith is not proven by what we say on Sunday—it's proven by what we do **on Monday, in the midst of trial, tension, and testing**. Just as a car cannot move forward without an engine, **faith cannot produce results without works**. Confession without action is empty. Belief without obedience is powerless. Faith that moves mountains is faith that first moves **us**.

In every generation, God seeks those who will put their faith to work—not just in word, but in deed. When we act upon what we believe, heaven responds. Divine provision meets us on the path of obedience. God does not honor passive faith; He honors active trust. That is the difference between a believer and a **faith-walker**. One talks about what God can do. The other moves, sacrifices, and lives as if the promise is already fulfilled. That kind of faith is **alive**, and that kind of faith pleases God.

Faith in Action: Real Models of the God Kind of Faith

Faith is not passive—it is active, visible, and powerful. When the God kind of faith is in operation, it produces undeniable results. Scripture provides vivid accounts where faith moved beyond the heart and mind, manifesting in tangible actions that aligned with God's Word and power. These examples not only demonstrate the principles of faith but also provide a model for how believers today can walk in bold expectation, confidence, and spiritual authority.

One of the most striking demonstrations of faith in action is found in the story of **the woman with the issue of blood**. According to Mark 5:27–29 (KJV), "When she had heard of Jesus, came in the press behind, and touched his garment. For she said, "If I may touch but his clothes, I shall be whole." This woman had endured twelve years of suffering, social isolation, and financial loss at the hands of physicians, yet her condition only grew worse. What changed everything was not just her desperation, but her declaration and her determination. The Amplified Bible emphasizes that she "kept saying" within herself, "If I only touch His garments, I will be healed." This repetition illustrates persistent faith—a heart that refused to be denied. She believed, she spoke, and she acted. Despite her weakness and the risk of being publicly shamed, she pressed through the crowd. That single touch, powered by faith, drew healing virtue from Jesus. He stopped and acknowledged her, not because of the physical contact, but because her **faith made a demand on the anointing**. Jesus confirmed this truth by saying, "Daughter, thy faith hath made thee whole" (Mark 5:34, KJV). Her healing was not accidental—it was faith in motion.

Similarly, we see faith come alive in the story of **the man with the withered hand** in Mark 3:3–5 (KJV). In a synagogue setting surrounded by religious critics, Jesus instructed the man, "Stand forth... Stretch forth thine hand." At that moment, the man could have hesitated, doubted, or waited to see a sign first—but instead, he responded immediately. His act of obedience activated his miracle. The scripture states, "And he stretched it out: and his hand was restored whole as the other." The power of this account lies in the simplicity and immediacy of action. Jesus did not lay hands on him or perform a visible ritual. The man's restoration was the direct result of doing what Jesus said, **without question or delay**. This illustrates that faith often requires us to take bold steps in moments that seem ordinary. Faith hears the Word and acts—even when it doesn't make natural sense.

Another profound example is found in the narrative of **the Roman centurion and his servant** in Matthew 8:5–10 (KJV). When Jesus offered to come to the centurion's house to heal his servant, the centurion stopped Him and declared, "Speak the word only, and my servant shall be healed." This declaration astounded Jesus. The centurion—a man of authority—recognized that Jesus operated under divine authority. Just as he commanded soldiers and they obeyed, he believed that Jesus only needed to **speak**, and healing would occur regardless of distance. Jesus responded by saying, "I have not found so great faith, no, not in Israel." What made this faith "great"? It was a combination of humility, understanding of authority, and absolute trust in the spoken word of Christ. The centurion's faith didn't require evidence or proximity—it rested solely on the reliability of Jesus' Word. This reminds us that **faith speaks, believes, and expects**, even when the answer has not yet manifested in the natural.

In each of these occurrences, we witness a recurring pattern: **belief in the heart, confession with the mouth, and obedience through action**. Whether it was the woman reaching, the man stretching, or the centurion speaking, faith was seen and heard. These stories reveal that the God kind of faith is not theoretical; it is practical. It presses through crowds. It stretches out crippled hands. It speaks bold declarations when the facts say otherwise. And most importantly, **it pleases God and causes heaven to respond.**

These patterns are not ancient relics of divine encounters. They are living testimonies, preserved by the Holy Spirit to show us how to walk by faith in our own lives today. Just like them, we must hear the Word, believe it, speak it, and act on it. And just like them, **our faith will make us whole**.

So, I ask... Is Faith the Key to Everything? Yes. Faith is the **key to everything** in the kingdom of God. Without it, we cannot please Him (Hebrews 11:6). With it, **we receive, overcome, and dominate**. We live. We love. We move mountains. Faith is not a feeling, but it is God's law. And just like gravity, it works for **anyone** who engages it. Whether in a hospital room, a courtroom, a classroom, or the middle of a crisis, faith releases heaven into earth.

Final Word: Arise in the Law of Faith

Child of God, the law has been established. Heaven is waiting. God has already given you the measure of faith. The question is: **will you use it?**

Let every doubt die. Let every excuse be buried. Rise in the power of the Law of Faith. Speak what God speaks. Believe what God says. Act on what He has promised.

The moment you cross the line from doubt to belief; you'll discover this truth: **God's power flows wherever His faith is alive.**

Walk boldly. Speak powerfully. Believe relentlessly. You are not waiting on God. God is waiting on **you** to believe

| 2 |

The Law of Faith II

"For we walk by faith, not by sight." — **2 Corinthians 5:7, KJV**

In every season of life, words matter. What you speak is not just a reflection of your thoughts—it is a declaration of your beliefs, your authority, and your alignment with heaven. Faith, when matured, does not remain silent. It speaks. It commands. It calls things into being. In this chapter, 'Faith That Speaks,' we explore how biblical faith transcends inner belief and becomes a vocal, creative force that transforms the atmosphere, releases divine power, and ushers in the promises of God. Through Scripture, real-life examples, and Spirit-led insight, you will be equipped to move from believing quietly to declaring boldly; because the kingdom responds to voices filled with faith.

Walking by faith is far more than a spiritual cliché—it is the foundational principle upon which the life of every believer must be built. The Apostle Paul reminded the church at Corinth that the believer's journey cannot be governed by physical sight, emotional responses, or worldly logic. Rather, the true walk of faith is governed by trust in the unseen, by a reliance on God's Word, and by a confidence in His character. This walk is not passive or automatic; it is a **moment-by-moment, day-by-day decision** to prioritize divine truth over temporary circumstances. The natural man is led by the senses—what he can see, touch, reason, and feel—but the spiritual man, reborn in Christ, lives by the **Law of Faith**, a law that transcends human limitations and taps into the realm of the supernatural.

Paul further explains this concept in **Romans 12:3 (KJV)**, writing, "God hath dealt to every man the measure of faith." This means that every believer is born again with a **divine deposit of faith**—a spiritual seed that, when nurtured, has the capacity to grow, expand, and produce kingdom-level results. However, this faith must be exercised and developed. Just as physical muscles grow through resistance and training, faith matures through hearing the Word, obeying God's instructions, and enduring life's trials with trust in the Lord. Scripture reveals that faith is not one-dimensional; it comes in various **measures**, **qualities**, and **manifestations** with each revealing the depth of a believer's spiritual maturity and alignment with God's purposes.

Little Faith: The Beginning of Trust

Faith, like any spiritual virtue, must begin somewhere. Little faith is often the first expression of belief that emerges in a believer's heart. In Matthew 6:30 (KJV), Jesus challenges His disciples' fear and anxiety about provision, saying, *"Wherefore, if God so clothe the grass of the field, which today is, and tomorrow is cast into the oven, shall he not much more clothe you, O ye of little faith?"* His words are not merely a gentle encouragement—they are a firm correction. The phrase "O ye of little faith" appears multiple times throughout the Gospels, always in moments when the disciples are overcome with worry, fear, or unbelief. It characterizes a level of faith that acknowledges God's existence but struggles to trust in His ongoing involvement, care, and reliability in everyday matters.

Jesus had just finished teaching about the futility of worry—highlighting how the Father feeds the birds and clothes the lilies—and He was directing His listeners to trust in the providence of a God who is both aware of and involved in the intimate details of their lives. Earlier in the same chapter, in Matthew 6:8 (KJV), Jesus said, *"For your Father knoweth what things ye have need of, before ye ask him."* This verse stresses the nature of our relationship with God—not just as Creator, but as Father, intimately aware of our needs even before we voice them. The issue, then, is not whether God knows or cares, but whether we believe that He is both willing and able to respond. Little faith struggles in this gap between believing in God and trusting God.

Little faith is often fragile and inconsistent. It is reactive—responding more to external conditions than to the internal conviction of God's Word. It tends to panic under pressure, questions in delay, and hesitates in the face of spiritual opposition. Little faith often asks, *"What if I fail?" "What if God doesn't come through?" "What if I'm not enough?"* These are the voices of fear that drown out the still, small voice of God's assurance. Jesus never condemned His disciples for having no faith at all in these moments, but He was clear that little faith is not enough to live victoriously in the kingdom. It may get us started, but it will not carry us through.

Theologically, little faith often arises from a limited understanding of God's character. It sees God as mighty in general but questions His willingness in the personal. This is why Jesus repeatedly taught about the Father's heart—He was building a bridge between the head knowledge of God's power and the heart knowledge of God's love. The transition from little faith to great faith comes when believers stop seeing God as distant and begin seeing Him as present, trustworthy, and involved in every detail of their lives.

In practical terms, little faith is common at the early stages of the Christian walk, but it is not meant to remain. It is the seed that must be watered with the Word, nurtured through prayer, and strengthened by spiritual discipline. God is patient with our growth, but He also expects us to grow. His desire is that our faith becomes robust, resilient, and deeply rooted in His promises. As Paul wrote in Romans 10:17, "Faith cometh by hearing, and hearing by the word of God." The more we hear, know, and apply the Word, the more our faith matures.

In the end, little faith is not a place of condemnation but a call to development. Jesus' words, though corrective, are also instructional. He shows us that while little faith may get us out of the boat, only maturing faith will keep us walking on the water. Therefore, the call of the believer is to grow from little faith to unwavering trust—not asking, "What if I fail?" but declaring confidently, "God cannot fail."

Great Faith: The Faith That Moves Heaven

Among all the remarkable displays of belief recorded in the Gospels, few are as striking as the encounter between Jesus and the Roman centurion found in Matthew 8:10 (KJV). The centurion, a Gentile and a military officer in the occupying Roman army, approaches Jesus not with arrogance or entitlement, but with humility and astounding spiritual insight. When requesting healing for his paralyzed and suffering servant, the centurion says to Jesus, *"speak the word only, and my servant shall be healed."* Jesus' response is one of awe: *"Verily I say unto you, I have not found so great faith, no, not in Israel."* This profound moment reveals a dimension of faith that transcends cultural boundaries, religious traditions, and natural reasoning. It unveils what Scripture calls "great faith"; a faith so mature, so confident in God's authority, that it astonishes even the Author and Finisher of our faith.

What made the centurion's faith "great" was not its emotion or eloquence, but its understanding of authority and its trust in the spoken Word. The centurion drew a direct parallel between his own role as a commander and Jesus' divine authority. Just as he could issue orders and expect immediate results from his subordinates, he believed that Jesus, who operated under the supreme authority of God, could simply speak a command and it would be fulfilled, even at a distance. He did not need Jesus to come physically to his home, lay hands on the servant, or perform a visible act. He trusted that Jesus' word alone had the same force, presence, and power as Jesus Himself. This is the essence of great faith: it does not require physical evidence to validate spiritual truth.

This kind of faith is built not on ritual, religion, or tradition, but on revelation. The centurion did not grow up in the synagogue, he was not raised under the Law of Moses, and he had no religious pedigree. Yet he saw something in Jesus that even many of the religious leaders and covenant-keeping Jews had missed: the absolute authority of His word. Great faith, therefore, is not determined by background, status, or title, but it is measured by the level of confidence one places in God's spoken word. Where little faith looks for signs, great faith rests in what God has already said.

Great faith stands as a model for the New Testament believer. It shows us that the Word of God is not merely instructional, however, it is creative, authoritative, and miraculous. When Jesus declared in John 6:63, "the words that I speak unto you, they are spirit, and they are life," He affirmed what the centurion already knew by revelation: that His words were alive, backed by heaven, and incapable of failing. Great faith takes God at His word, not waiting for a feeling, a manifestation, or a confirmation. It believes first, speaks in agreement, and then sees the results.

Practically speaking, great faith is what empowers believers to stand firm in trials, speak life over impossible situations, and believe in healing, provision, and deliverance—even when there is no visible sign of change. It does not panic when the answer is delayed, nor does it diminish when circumstances contradict the promise. It is steadfast, immovable, and fully persuaded, just as Abraham was, that "what [God] had promised, He was able also to perform" (Romans 4:21, KJV).

Jesus' astonishment at the centurion's faith is telling. It suggests that such faith is rare, even among those who claim to believe. And yet, this passage also confirms that such faith is accessible to anyone, regardless of background; but will you choose to trust in the Word without hesitation. Great faith is not the exclusive domain of apostles or prophets—it belongs to the one who simply believes that when God speaks, it is done.

Strong Faith: Resilient Trust in the Face of Delay

In Romans 4:20 (KJV), the Apostle Paul offers a profound tribute to the unwavering trust of Abraham, stating, *"He staggered not at the promise of God through unbelief; but was strong in faith, giving glory to God."* These words are more than an honor; they are a blueprint for what it means to possess strong faith. Abraham, often called the "father of faith," was given a divine promise that defied every natural law: that he and his wife Sarah would conceive a son in their old age. By the time the promise was fulfilled, Abraham was nearly 100 years old, and Sarah was long past childbearing years. Yet, despite what he saw in the mirror, despite Sarah's barrenness, and despite the years of silence from heaven, Abraham's faith did not waver. He did not stagger; but stood firm.

Strong faith is marked by its resilience in waiting. It is not faith that simply believes at the beginning of the journey but continues to believe in the middle of uncertainty, when the promise appears delayed, and the evidence is scarce. Abraham's body, as Paul notes in Romans 4:19, was "now dead," and Sarah's womb was likewise lifeless. But Abraham's focus was not on his condition; it was on God's character. He trusted not in what he could do but in what God had said. Strong faith, therefore, is not faith in favorable outcomes; it is faith in the unchanging nature of God.

What makes this faith "strong" is not the absence of pressure, but the refusal to buckle under it. Strong faith grows in adversity, not apart from it. It is refined in silence, tested in the waiting room of life, and strengthened by resisting doubt. The Greek word used in Romans 4:20 (NKJV) for "staggered not" (diakrinō) implies hesitation or internal conflict. Abraham's faith did not alternate between belief and unbelief. His inner man was steadfast, convinced that delay did not mean denial, and silence did not mean abandonment. While his natural circumstances screamed "impossible," his spirit whispered "God is faithful."

Moreover, Paul tells us that Abraham “gave glory to God” in the midst of his waiting. This is one of the most powerful characteristics of strong faith—it worships while waiting. It praises before the manifestation. It exalts God not based on what is seen, but on what is promised. Worship is not just an act of gratitude; it is an act of warfare and declaration. Every time Abraham lifted his voice to glorify God, he was strengthening his faith and silencing unbelief.

Spiritually, strong faith represents the maturity that comes from an ongoing relationship with God. It is faith that remembers past victories and rehearses past faithfulness. It is not naive or blind—it is informed by God’s nature and reinforced by history with Him. Abraham’s strong faith did not eliminate questions, but it refused to let questions lead to doubt. Strong faith rests in the fact that God is both able and willing to perform His word, even if the when and how remain undisclosed.

This kind of faith challenges today’s believers to remain anchored in the Word of God, especially in seasons where promises are yet to be fulfilled. It teaches us to resist the urge to create our own timelines or force our own outcomes. Instead, strong faith invites us to wait with hope, to praise with purpose, and to believe with the conviction that God always finishes what He starts (Philippians 1:6). It is the type of faith that does not need to see the rain cloud to start building the ark.

Strong faith does not emerge from comfort, but is shaped in the fires of adversity and contradiction.. It is the kind of faith that brings glory to God not because of what is received, but because of the relentless trust that He will deliver in His perfect timing. Abraham's story reminds us that when faith holds its ground, the promise will come, and the glory will belong to God alone.

Vain Faith: A Faith Without Substance

While faith is essential to the Christian life, not all faith is authentic or acceptable before God. The Apostle Paul issues a sobering warning in 1 Corinthians 15:14 (KJV): *"And if Christ be not risen, then is our preaching vain, and your faith is also vain."* This verse strikes at the heart of what makes faith meaningful, its object and its foundation. Paul is making it clear that faith must be rooted in truth—specifically, the resurrection of Jesus Christ. Without the resurrection, the entire gospel collapses, and faith becomes an exercise in futility. This kind of "vain faith" is not simply weak or immature; it is misplaced, empty, and powerless. It may be sincere, but it is sincerely wrong.

Vain faith is often faith in form rather than in substance. It places confidence in religious rituals, denominational loyalty, or cultural Christianity rather than in the living Word of God. It may be driven by emotion, habit, or tradition, but it lacks the transformative power of faith grounded in truth and led by the Spirit. Vain faith gives the appearance of spirituality; sounding eloquent in speech, displaying outward devotion, and participating in religious activity, but yet it bears no fruit. Jesus warned of this kind of faith when He quoted Isaiah, saying, *"This people draweth nigh unto me with their mouth, and honoureth me with their lips; but their heart is far from me"* (Matthew 15:8, KJV). Vain faith is cosmetic—it looks alive on the surface but is disconnected from obedience and intimacy with God.

Vain faith can quietly lead us astray, giving the impression that all is well with our soul—even when our foundation isn't truly rooted in Christ. Vain faith is also dangerous because it provides a false sense of security. It convinces people that proximity to religious practices is equivalent to a relationship with Christ. It numbs the conscience while leaving the soul untouched. In this way, vain faith is not just ineffective but it is deceptive. It mimics the real while keeping the believer from experiencing the supernatural life available through genuine, Spirit-led faith. Where true faith results in transformation, endurance, and spiritual authority, vain faith results in stagnation, confusion, and eventual disillusionment when challenges arise and there is no power to stand.

Furthermore, vain faith cannot endure hardship because it is built on shifting sand. When tested by trials, persecution, or spiritual warfare, it collapses. Jesus illustrates this truth in the parable of the wise and foolish builders (Matthew 7:24–27). The house built on sand looked sturdy until the storm came. In the same way, vain faith may appear legitimate during times of peace, but its hollowness is exposed to adversity. This is why Paul was so adamant in warning the Corinthian church: if Christ is not risen, your faith is not just weak but it is worthless.

In practical terms, vain faith is often seen in believers who know religious language but lack personal conviction. It's seen in those who attend church but are unmoved by the gospel, who recite Scripture but do not apply it, who profess Christ but resist surrender. Such faith offers no power, no transformation, and no eternal reward. It is like a lamp without oil; prepared in appearance but lacking the substance to sustain light.

Vain faith is a counterfeit. It serves as a reminder that not all belief is saving belief, and not all conviction is rooted in truth. True, living faith must be anchored in the finished work of Jesus Christ, fed by the Word of God, and evidenced by obedience and spiritual fruit. As James reminds us, *"faith without works is dead"* (James 2:17, KJV). And as Paul implies faith without resurrection is vain. The believer is therefore called not only to have faith but to ensure that their faith is authentic, active, and aligned with the living Christ.

Bold Faith: Faith That Dares to Speak and Act

Bold faith is the kind of faith that refuses to remain silent or hidden in the face of opposition. It is not passive or timid, nor is it reckless or self-exalting. Rather, bold faith is the courageous and confident expression of a believer who knows who they are in Christ and walks in the authority of God's Word. The Apostle Paul affirms this in 1 Timothy 3:13 (KJV), stating, *"For they that have used the office of a deacon well purchase to themselves a good degree, and great boldness in the faith which is in Christ Jesus."* Here, boldness is not presented as a personality trait—it is a spiritual reward earned through faithful service, obedience, and character development. Those who serve well and walk uprightly gain not only respect but also increased confidence in their spiritual authority.

Bold faith is rooted in spiritual identity and intimacy with God. It does not arise from self-confidence but from God-confidence—an unwavering belief that God's Word is true, His promises are sure, and His power is greater than any threat or opposition. Bold faith allows believers to pray audacious prayers, speak truth in difficult environments, and stand firm in moments of intense spiritual warfare. In the book of Acts, we see this in the apostles who, filled with the Holy Ghost, "spake the word of God with boldness" (Acts 4:31, KJV). Their courage was not natural but was supernatural, birthed from time in God's presence and a deep conviction that obedience was more important than personal safety.

This kind of faith is both vocal and visible. It speaks the Word of God with clarity and conviction, even when it contradicts culture or provokes criticism. It stands visibly for righteousness in a world increasingly hostile to truth. Bold faith does not retreat when challenged—it rises to the occasion, confronting fear, injustice, demonic resistance, and spiritual apathy with authority. It is the faith of Elijah on Mount Carmel, confronting false prophets and calling down fire from heaven (1 Kings 18). It is the faith of Esther who declared, "If I perish, I perish" (Esther 4:16), stepping into danger to fulfill her divine assignment. It is the faith of the early church who rejoiced in being counted worthy to suffer for the name of Jesus.

Bold faith flows from an understanding of the believer's access to God and their position in Christ. Hebrews 4:16 urges us to "come boldly unto the throne of grace," not with fear, but with full assurance that we are welcomed and empowered. When believers understand that they are sons and daughters of the Highest, they do not approach life's challenges as victims—they step forward as ambassadors, speaking and acting on heaven's behalf. This boldness is not arrogance; it is holy confidence, sanctified through surrender and empowered by the Spirit.

Practically, bold faith is essential in today's spiritual climate. It is the kind of faith that declares healing in the face of a negative diagnosis, that intercedes for cities and nations in the midst of moral decay, and that confronts compromise within the church with love and truth. It challenges systems of injustice, advocates for the vulnerable, and refuses to be silent when God calls His people to speak. In every generation, God has raised up bold believers, not because they were fearless by nature, but because their fear of God outweighed their fear of man.

Remember, bold faith is the faith that takes risks for righteousness, knowing that God honors courage rooted in obedience. It is not content to whisper in the shadows, but it speaks, acts, and advances the kingdom. In a world filled with intimidation and spiritual compromise, bold faith stands as a powerful witness that the God we serve is still speaking, still saving, and still moving through those who dare to believe and obey without hesitation.

Dead Faith: A Belief That Bears No Fruit

In the epistle of James, the Holy Spirit offers one of the most direct and sobering indictments of inauthentic faith: **faith without works is dead**. In **James 2:17 (KJV)**, it reads, *"Even so faith, if it hath not works, is dead, being alone."* This is not a mild warning—it is a theological verdict. Dead faith is faith that **exists in word but not in deed**; it may agree with God intellectually, but it is **devoid of action, obedience, and spiritual productivity**. It speaks of belief but lives in contradiction. It has the form of godliness but denies the power thereof (2 Timothy 3:5). James doesn't say this kind of faith is weak or immature, but he calls it **dead**, implying that it has no life, no power, and no value in advancing the kingdom of God.

This form of faith may sound pious or appear religious, but it is inactive **and ineffective**. It does not move the heart of God because it does not first move the heart of the believer. **Dead faith produces no fruit**—not in character, not in relationships, and not in spiritual outcomes. It remains **detached from transformation**, content with confession but unwilling to embrace conviction. It says "Amen" on Sunday but compromises on Monday. It agrees that Jesus is Lord but resists surrendering daily life to His authority.

James strengthens his point by offering a stark illustration in **verse 26**, saying, *"For as the body without the spirit is dead, so faith without works is dead also."* A body may look intact outwardly, but if it is lifeless—devoid of breath and motion—it is functionally useless. In the same way, **faith without corresponding action is faith in name only**. Verse 20 further asks, *"But wilt thou know, O vain man, that faith without works is dead?"* This rhetorical question cuts to the heart, calling out the empty religiosity of those who claim belief but show no evidence of obedience. Such faith is **spiritually stagnant**—it does not grow, reproduce, or bear witness to the transformative power of the gospel.

James is not suggesting that work earns salvation, but rather that **genuine faith produces visible obedience**. A tree is not a tree because it bears fruit, but the fruit is the evidence that it is alive. Similarly, good works are not the root of salvation, but they are the **fruit** of a faith that is alive and authentic. The danger of dead faith lies in its deception—it can cause individuals to believe they are spiritually secure while they remain **disconnected from the life of God**.

In today's church, dead faith can be seen in those who recite Scripture but resist submission, who attend church services faithfully but neglect the weightier matters of the Word—justice, mercy, humility, and love. It manifests in a **faith that talks loudly but lives passively**, one that acknowledges God with the lips but denies Him with lifestyle. Dead faith is content with appearance over substance, performance over purity, and attendance over intimacy.

Finally, dead faith is not a neutral condition—it is a **dangerous replica.** It numbs the conscience while leaving the heart unchanged. It does not inspire action, nor does it provoke repentance. Most critically, it robs the believer of the power, purpose, and presence that come with a life fully yielded to Christ. In a world desperate for living witnesses of God's truth, **dead faith fails to testify**.

The call from James is urgent and clear: **faith must be lived out, not just declared**. Real faith steps out, speaks up, sacrifices, and serves. It aligns the heart with heaven and translates belief into bold, consistent obedience. If faith is truly alive, it will be seen in action—and where there is no action, there is no life.

Holy Faith: The Faith Set Apart for God's Purposes

In a time of moral drift, spiritual confusion, and increasing compromise, the call to cultivate holy faith has never been more urgent. In Jude 1:20 (KJV), the Apostle Jude writes with apostolic urgency: *"But ye, beloved, building up yourselves on your most holy faith, praying in the Holy Ghost."* This brief but powerful command highlights both the sacredness and the intentionality of true biblical faith. Jude distinguishes "most holy faith" not as an ordinary belief, but as a consecrated trust—a faith that is set apart, pure in motive, protected from pollution, and deeply anchored in the presence and power of God. It is not a passive possession, but something that must be actively built up, nurtured, and sustained in a lifestyle of intimacy with the Holy Spirit.

The phrase "most holy faith" indicates a qualitative difference from generic belief. It speaks of a faith that has been refined by fire, matured by testing, and empowered by divine communion. This type of faith is rooted not just in doctrine but in devotion—it is cultivated through intentional spiritual disciplines such as fervent prayer, persistent worship, and immersion in the Word of God. Jude connects this faith directly to "praying in the Holy Ghost," reminding us that holy faith is sustained by a life of Spirit-led intercession and spiritual sensitivity. It thrives in the secret place and is strengthened through fellowship with the Spirit, who searches the deep things of God and intercedes according to His perfect will (Romans 8:26–27 KJV).

Holy faith is untainted by the world, unaffected by popular opinion, and unshaken by cultural compromise. It does not conform to the patterns of this world (Romans 12:2); instead, it holds fast to the will of God even when it costs something. It resists doubt, discerns deception, and defies discouragement. Where ordinary faith may falter under pressure or shift with popular opinion, holy faith is unmovable, anchored in divine truth and governed by spiritual discernment. It is clean because it is consecrated. It is durable because it is deeply rooted. And it is powerful because it is God-empowered.

This level of faith is also missional in nature. Holy faith does not exist for self-preservation; it exists for kingdom advancement. It is the kind of faith that anchors spiritual leaders, fuels revival, and births miracles. It is the kind of faith that enables prophets to speak truth to power, pastors to shepherd with integrity, intercessors to groan in the Spirit, and believers to stand firm in trials without compromising their convictions. Holy faith births movements, shapes nations, and carries the mantle of transformation because it is connected to the very heartbeat of God.

Furthermore, Jude's instruction to "build up yourselves" underscores the personal responsibility each believer carries. This faith is not inherited by tradition, delegated by leadership, or sustained by mere association with the church. It must be built—brick by brick, moment by moment—through intentional obedience, sacrificial worship, and relentless pursuit of God's presence. Holy faith grows as we invest in spiritual formation, remain teachable, and yield continually to the leading of the Holy Spirit.

In essence, holy faith is both a posture and a pursuit. It is a posture of surrender to God's will and a pursuit of His presence above all else. It is the distinguishing mark of a mature believer—someone who not only believes God can, but lives daily in alignment with who God is. In a world where diluted faith is common and superficial faith is celebrated; holy faith stands apart. It is deep, it is reverent, and it is empowered by heaven.

The God Kind of Faith: Faith That Creates and Commands

Among all the expressions of faith revealed in Scripture, the God kind of faith stands as the highest and most powerful form—a faith that not only responds to God but acts like God. In Mark 11:23 (KJV), Jesus offers one of the most radical and empowering declarations in the New Testament: *"For verily I say unto you, That whosoever shall say unto this mountain, Be thou removed, and be thou cast into the sea; and shall not doubt in his heart, but shall believe that those things which he saith shall come to pass; he shall have whatsoever he saith."* This is not hyperbole. It is a divine invitation into the realm of faith that creates, commands, and transforms. It is the faith that not only believes in the supernatural, it unleashes it.

The God kind of faith, often referred to as creative or commanding faith, is the faith that originates from God's own nature. In the beginning, as recorded in Genesis 1, God did not consult the elements; He spoke, and the elements obeyed. *"And God said, Let there be light: and there was light"* (Genesis 1:3, KJV). God spoke into the void, and creation responded. This is not faith that reacts to circumstances—it is faith that shapes circumstances. It does not wait for evidence to believe; it believes in order to create evidence. This is the essence of the God kind of faith—it initiates change by the spoken Word, grounded in absolute confidence that what is spoken according to God's will must come to pass.

Jesus demonstrated this faith consistently during His earthly ministry. He spoke to storms, and they calmed. He spoke to dead bodies, and they rose. He spoke to trees, and they withered. Every time, He modeled a faith that acts with authority, fully aligned with the will of the Father and void of hesitation or doubt. This is the kind of faith Jesus was teaching His disciples to walk in—not just a believing faith, but a declaring faith, one that speaks to mountains and expects movement.

The God kind of faith is rooted in the principle that words are containers of power. Proverbs 18:21 declares, *"Death and life are in the power of the tongue,"* and Mark 11:23 confirms that what we say; if believed in the heart and spoken in faith, can alter natural reality. This is not "name-it-and-claim-it" theology detached from God's will; rather, it is Word-based, Spirit-led declaration that aligns with heaven's agenda. The God kind of faith refuses to entertain doubt, because it is anchored in God's unchanging nature and the authority of His promises. It is fully persuaded that if God's Word says it, then that Word carries the legal right and spiritual force to manifest it.

The God kind of faith transforms how believers approach everything—from prayer to problems, from crisis to calling. This kind of faith does not settle for survival; it commands advancement. It does not merely hope for breakthrough; it declares breakthrough with conviction. It does not beg God to move; it moves with God. This faith speaks healing in the face of sickness, provision in the face of lack, and peace in the face of chaos. It is a faith that does not flinch at the impossible, because it is rooted in a God for whom nothing is impossible.

Furthermore, this type of faith is the mature believer's inheritance. Jesus began Mark 11:23 with the words, "Verily I say unto you," emphasizing the certainty and accessibility of this truth to anyone who believes. He did not restrict it to apostles, prophets, or spiritual elites. He said, "Whosoever shall say unto this mountain..." Whosoever includes every believer who will step into a place of spiritual confidence and alignment with the Word. This is not arrogance but kingdom authority in action.

The God kind of faith is not a passive attitude, but an active force. It is the creative, commanding faith that flows from knowing who God is, who we are in Him, and what His Word has already declared. It is the faith that causes heaven to invade earth, that calls things which be not as though they were (Romans 4:17), and that releases the supernatural in ordinary places. This is the faith that Jesus lived by, taught, and entrusted to His followers. It is the highest dimension of faith, and it remains available to all who will believe, speak, and refuse to doubt.

Faith That Speaks: The Voice of Supernatural Authority

In the life of every believer, faith must mature beyond silent belief; but become faith that speaks. The God kind of faith is not passive; it is vocal. It declares the promises of God; commands change and confronts darkness. This speaking faith is not wishful thinking or positive affirmation. It is the verbal release of divine truth grounded in revelation and empowered by the Holy Spirit.

Jesus Himself modeled this in every area of His ministry. In Mark 11:23 (NKJV), He said, "Whoever says to this mountain, 'Be removed and be cast into the sea,' and does not doubt in his heart, but believes that those things he says will be done, he will have whatever he says." This is not metaphorical language, but it is a literal spiritual law. Jesus did not teach His disciples to silently wish mountains away. He taught them to speak with boldness, believing that what they said in alignment with God's Will would come to pass.

The Amplified Bible expands the verse: "I assure you and most solemnly say to you, whoever says to this mountain, 'Be lifted up and thrown into the sea!' and does not doubt in his heart but believes that what he says is going to take place, it will be done for him [in accordance with God's will]." In other words, our words must agree with what is established in heaven. Speaking faith is not emotional chatter, but it is intentional declaration rooted in covenantal truth.

Consider the woman with the issue of blood in Mark 5:28 (NKJV): "For she said, 'If only I may touch His clothes, I shall be made well.'" Her miracle did not begin with the touch—it began with what she said. The Amplified Version adds, "She kept saying, 'If I only touch His outer robe, I will be healed.'" Her persistent, internal confession gave birth to external transformation.

Another example is found in Luke 7:7 (The Message Bible) when the Roman centurion tells Jesus, “Just give the order and my servant will be fine.” Jesus marvels at his words, stating, “I’ve yet to come across this kind of simple trust anywhere in Israel.” The centurion didn’t need physical evidence—he only needed the spoken word. This is the hallmark of speaking faith: trusting that God's Word, once released, is enough to activate the miraculous.

When facing challenges in health, finances, family, or identity, silence is not a spiritual strategy. Proverbs 18:21 (AMP) tells us, “Death and life are in the power of the tongue, and those who love it and indulge it will eat its fruit and bear the consequences of their words.” This means your words are not neutral, but they are either planting seeds of faith or fear, life or defeat. Faith that speaks is careful not to echo problems, it proclaims promises.

During personal trials, speaking faith is what sustains and advances the believer. When David faced Goliath, he didn’t just believe in his heart—he declared, “This day the Lord will deliver you into my hand” (1 Samuel 17:46, NKJV). He spoke the outcome before the battle even began.

Speaking faith also aligns with praying in the Spirit. 1 Corinthians 2:13 (AMP) says, “We also speak these things, not in words taught or supplied by human wisdom, but those taught by the Spirit, combining and interpreting spiritual thoughts with spiritual words [for those being guided by the Holy Spirit].” Faith that speaks is not guided by flesh or circumstance, but it is empowered by divine utterance.

Silence may preserve dignity but spoken faith releases destiny. It is not enough to believe quietly—your voice must agree with God's Word. Faith that speaks is the language of victory, the vehicle of creative power, and the signal to the enemy that the believer is fully persuaded.

So, open your mouth. Speak the Word. Declare the promise. Rebuke the storm. Bless your body. Command your breakthrough. As it is written in 2 Corinthians 4:13 (NKJV): "And since we have the same spirit of faith... we also believe and therefore speak."

Faith: A Living Force for a Kingdom Life

Faith is never meant to be static, stagnant, or situational. It is a living, breathing, and continually evolving force that must be nurtured in the believer's life through consistent intimacy with God and unwavering obedience to His Word. Far from being a one-time decision or passive belief, faith is a spiritual journey that deepens with every act of surrender, matures with every test, and strengthens through every trial. Whether a believer begins with little faith—marked by uncertainty—or advances into strong, bold, or holy faith, the progression is designed by God to lead us into the realm of the God kind of faith. This is the dimension of faith that does more than sustain the believer—it transforms lives, shifts spiritual atmospheres, and collaborates with heaven to bring God's will into visible manifestation on the earth.

The measure of faith imparted to every believer at salvation (Romans 12:3) is not the final destination; it is the divine starting point. God never intended for us to remain at the level of "just enough to believe." Rather, He calls us to grow from faith to faith (Romans 1:17), building layer upon layer of trust, revelation, and action. Just as physical muscles grow through resistance and exercise, spiritual faith grows through obedience, prayer, and application of truth. Every time we choose to believe when doubt beckons, every time we speak God's Word when circumstances suggest silence, and every time we act in obedience when it's inconvenient or uncomfortable, our faith is strengthened and refined.

Mature faith is the God kind of faith; it is the faith that speaks with authority, acts with confidence, and produces results. It no longer depends on the visible to affirm the invisible. It does not ask whether God will show up; it moves forward knowing that God is already present. This kind of faith releases healing, calls forth provision, opens doors, and changes destinies. It does not simply react to the world; it recreates it in alignment with heaven's decree. It glorifies the Father not only through words but through demonstrated power—by producing fruit, performing works aligned with His Spirit, and fulfilling the unique assignment given to every believer in the body of Christ.

The Law of Faith is not a doctrinal concept to be memorized, nor is it a spiritual option for the "super anointed." It is a way of life—a divine operating system—for all who dare to believe. To walk by faith is to walk in step with the heartbeat of heaven, carrying divine authority into earthly realms. It is a daily decision to trust God completely, speak boldly, act courageously, and live intentionally knowing that faith is the currency of the kingdom, and those who live by it will lack no good thing. When faith is alive and active, impossibilities crumble, God is glorified, and the believer becomes a vessel through which heaven touches earth.

The Call to Speak Life

This chapter affirms a timeless truth: faith that remains silent may believe, but faith that speaks receives. The power of our confession lies not in emotional enthusiasm, but in spiritual authority. When you speak God's Word, you are not just echoing Scripture—you are enforcing heaven's will on earth. From the centurion's command to the woman with the issue of blood, speaking faith brought supernatural results. Now it's your turn. As you meditate on these truths, remember that your words are not idle—they are instruments of dominion. Speak the Word. Declare His promises. Release heaven into every area of your life. For in this season, your victory is voice-activated.

Final Saying – "From Measure to Mastery: Let Your Faith Grow Stronger"

"Faith is not just something you possess; it's something you practice. The measure you've been given was never meant to sit idle.

Feed it, stretch it, speak through it, and watch it grow—until it no longer responds to what you see, but only to what God has said."

| 3 |

The Battle is Not Yours: Fighting the Good Fight of Faith

"Faith is your weapon, your shield, and your breath—fight with it or fall without it."

Faith Is the Fight-You were not saved into serenity—you were saved into a spiritual war. The moment you chose Christ, you enlisted in a battle not for land, but for legacy, not for riches, but for righteousness. But here is the divine advantage: God never intended for you to fight alone. He gave you the most powerful weapon in your spiritual arsenal faith. Faith is not only your victory, but your lifeline. Without it, you suffocate in fear, doubt, and defeat. With it, you rise in authority, truth, and triumph. In this chapter, you'll discover how faith functions as both shield and sword in spiritual warfare. You'll see how the "good fight" is won not by striving in the flesh but by standing in the Spirit. This battle is not yours; it's the Lord's. But He fights through your faith.

The believer's journey is not a stroll through fields of ease and emotional comfort—it is a spiritual warzone where battles are waged daily for the mind, the will, and the soul. This walk with God demands more than church attendance and Christian clichés; it requires faith as a spiritual life source. Just as oxygen is indispensable to the body, faith is indispensable to the spirit. Without it, the Christian life is void of power, vision, and victory. Faith is not a suggestion, nor is it an accessory to the Christian experience. According to Scripture, it is the foundation and fuel of everything God calls us to do.

Paul reinforces this in 2 Corinthians 5:7, where he declares, *"For we walk by faith, not by sight."* This is not symbolic language; it is a call to live based on God's promises, not our perceptions. In Romans 1:17, Paul reiterates, *"The just shall live by faith,"* emphasizing that righteousness is not sustained by behavior alone but by continued belief in God's faithfulness. The writer of Hebrews concurs, stating that without faith, it is impossible to please God (Hebrews 11:6). These verses collectively form a doctrinal cornerstone: faith is not just part of the journey, but it is the journey.

Furthermore, in 1 Timothy 6:12, Paul charges believers to *"Fight the good fight of faith."* This declaration confirms that faith is not a passive possession; it is a spiritual weapon of warfare. The "good fight" is not against people, politics, or personal enemies; it is a fight to hold on to what God has said, to resist fear and deception, and to stand firm in the face of every storm. Faith enables the believer to engage in battle not with clenched fists but with confident trust in the One who fights for them.

In today's world where trials are constant, spiritual warfare is real, and temptations are many, faith is the very breath of the believer's soul. Without it, the Christian becomes spiritually suffocated, unable to see beyond the present difficulty or trust in God's future deliverance. With it, however, the believer rises with strength, clarity, and divine authority to overcome every obstacle. Faith is not optional; it is essential. It is the only way to live victoriously, to please God continually, and to finish this journey triumphantly.

The Highest Level of Faith: Taking God at His Word

The highest level of faith is not measured by outward miracles, emotional highs, or the visible manifestation of answered prayers. Rather, it is measured by an unshakable conviction that God's Word is true—always, absolutely, and eternally. This kind of faith does not waver in the face of uncertainty, nor does it seek external confirmation before believing. It believes because God has spoken, and for the believer, that is enough. At this level, faith operates with the understanding that the Word of God is the final authority, overriding symptoms, statistics, circumstances, and even personal experiences.

This is not blind faith; it is suggestive faith; faith that is born not of emotional impulse but of spiritual understanding. According to Hebrews 4:12–13, the Word of God is not just an inspired document or ancient text—it is alive, powerful, and discerning. The King James Version (KJV) reads: *"For the word of God is quick, and powerful, and sharper than any two-edged sword... and is a discerner of the thoughts and intents of the heart."* Here, the word "quick" means alive indicating that Scripture carries with it the same vitality that created the universe. It is not a historical record of what God once said; it is the living voice of God still speaking.

God's Word is not passive; it is working, moving, and producing results wherever it is received by faith. It has energy. It performs divine surgery in the soul—cutting away doubt, diagnosing motives, and making room for truth to grow. *"For the Word that God speaks is alive and full of power [making it active, operative, energizing, and effective]. It is sharper than any two-edged sword... and able to judge the very thoughts and intentions of the heart."*

The Message Bible captures the same truth in vivid, contemporary language: *"God means what he says. What he says goes. His powerful Word is sharp as a surgeon's scalpel, cutting through everything, whether doubt or defense, laying us open to listen and obey."* This translation paints a picture of the Word not only exposing the deep places of our hearts but also skillfully and precisely addressing the very things that hinder our spiritual progress. Nothing escapes it. No argument or emotional barrier can hide from its reach.

What does this mean for the believer walking in the highest level of faith? It means that our confidence is not in outcomes, but in God's character and His Word. It means we do not need to see physical change before believing we are healed. We do not need to feel goosebumps to believe we are delivered. We do not need favorable reports to confess that we are victorious. We take God at His Word—period. That is the essence of mature, mountain-moving, miracle-working faith.

This Word—the same Word that framed the worlds (Hebrews 11:3)—is the Word that sustains our lives. The moment a believer moves from needing signs to simply resting in Scripture, they step into the realm of faith where God's Word becomes more real than their senses. They no longer require constant reassurance or visible evidence. They trust the Word because they know its source: the unchanging, all-powerful, and eternally faithful God.

Faith at this level is not emotional; it is positional. It declares, "God said it. I believe it. That settles it." It treats God's Word like a contract that cannot be broken and like a sword that never dulls. It recognizes that every Word from God contains within it the power to fulfill itself (Isaiah 55:11 KJV). This is the faith that brings rest to the soul, clarity to the mind, and victory in every spiritual battle. It is the faith that pleases God (Hebrews 11:6) and shakes the gates of hell.

Understanding the New Birth

When a believer is born again, a supernatural transfer takes place. Colossians 1:12–14 (KJV) says, *"Giving thanks unto the Father, which hath made us meet to be partakers of the inheritance of the saints in light: who hath delivered us from the power of darkness, and hath translated us into the kingdom of his dear Son."* The Bible explains that He "has drawn us to Himself out of the control and dominion of darkness and has transferred us into the kingdom of the Son of His love."

Let's break that down:

- "Who hath delivered us" means it is already done—not something God will do someday, but something already completed in the finished work of Christ.
- The word "power" in this passage is the Greek word *exousia*, which translates to authority.
- The term "darkness" refers to everything Satan represents—ignorance, sin, fear, bondage, destruction, and spiritual blindness.

At the moment of new birth, the believer was rescued out of Satan's jurisdiction and legally relocated into the Kingdom of Light. We no longer live under the authority of the devil—he has no legal claim over our lives. Yet, to walk in this reality requires faith that believes, speaks, and acts on the truth of the Word.

Walking in Authority: Living Set Apart, Standing Victorious

To walk in authority as a believer is to understand and act upon the spiritual position we have in Christ. Authority is not merely a concept—it is a kingdom mandate grounded in revelation, sealed by the blood of Jesus, and activated through faith and obedience. Jesus unveils the reality of spiritual warfare in John 10:10 (KJV) when He declares, *"The thief cometh not, but for to steal, and to kill, and to destroy: I am come that they might have life, and that they might have it more abundantly."* This verse clearly outlines the agenda of the enemy: Satan is a thief, whose mission is rooted in destruction, deception, and death. However, the second half of this verse reveals the counter-strategy of Christ—He came to impart not just life, but abundant life, overflowing with purpose, power, and peace. The believer, therefore, is not left defenseless. We have been given the tools to override the devil's agenda and live in victory.

One of the most powerful weapons in this spiritual battle is revealed in Revelation 12:11 (KJV): *"And they overcame him by the blood of the Lamb, and by the word of their testimony..."* The victory over the enemy does not come through human effort, talent, or emotional strength—it comes through the blood of Jesus and the bold declaration of what God has done. The blood of the Lamb is not symbolic; it is a legal transaction that forever disarmed Satan's power and secured our redemption (Colossians 2:15). But that victory must be enforced through our testimony—speaking the truth of who Christ is, what He has done, and who we now are in Him. The Amplified Bible expands this verse, saying, *"They did not love their life and renounce their faith even when faced with death."* This highlights a key trait of overcoming faith: it remains unshaken under pressure. True authority does not retreat in the face of adversity—it stands firm, knowing the outcome is already determined by the blood.

In order to walk in authority, we must also walk in separation from darkness. 2 Corinthians 6:14–17 (KJV) presents a direct challenge to believers: *"What fellowship hath righteousness with unrighteousness? and what communion hath light with darkness?"* The Apostle Paul calls for a radical separation—not as an act of legalism, but as an expression of covenantal alignment. When we were born again, we were transferred out of the kingdom of darkness and brought into the kingdom of God's dear Son (Colossians 1:13). To continue walking in victory, we must reject the values, attitudes, and systems of darkness that once held us captive. The Amplified version deepens this command: *"For we are the temple of the living God; just as God said: 'I will dwell among them and walk among them; and I will be their God, and they shall be My people.' So come out from among unbelievers and be separate, says the Lord, and do not touch what is unclean."*

This is not about earning salvation—it's about protecting and enforcing our spiritual authority. Authority thrives in purity. When we align ourselves with the holiness of God, we silence the accusations of the enemy and stand in the full backing of heaven. The moment we compromise and mingle light with darkness; we weaken our stance and open the door to spiritual oppression. Separation is not a punishment—it is a position of power.

Practical Application: Living at the Highest Level of Faith

- **Speak what God says—even when your senses argue otherwise.**
  Example: When symptoms appear, declare: *"By His stripes I am healed"* (Isaiah 53:5) and believe it from the heart (Mark 11:23–24).

- **Act like God's Word is true—even if results are not immediate.**
  Example: If God's Word says you have peace, resist anxiety and walk in inner calm by praying and standing on Philippians 4:6–7.

- **Refuse to be intimidated by darkness.**
  Example: If fear or temptation arises, say out loud: *"I have been delivered from the authority of darkness and translated into the kingdom of God's dear Son."* (Colossians 1:13)

- **Declare your victory boldly.**
  Example: Use Revelation 12:11 to proclaim: *"I overcome by the blood of Jesus and the word of my testimony."* Then testify out loud what God has done and what He will do.

Living in the Highest Level of Faith: Ruling Through Revelation

The highest level of faith is faith that knows God, believes His Word without compromise, and acts with boldness, even in the unseen. It is faith that says, "If God said it, then it is so." This faith understands that God's Word is more than a sacred text—it is a living revelation, infused with divine authority and creative power. When we walk in this faith, we don't just survive life—we reign in life (Romans 5:17). The battle is not about who is stronger—Christ has already won. The real question is: will we rise up and take God at His Word?

The highest level of faith is not merely about belief—it is about conviction, confidence, and courageous action rooted in the unshakable nature of God's Word. This is faith that knows God personally, trusts His promises without wavering, and steps forward with bold obedience, even when there is no physical evidence to support the promise. It is the kind of faith that declares, *"If God said it, then it is already settled."* There is no negotiation, no need for validation from others, and no hesitation based on the natural realm. This level of faith is not blind—it is enlightened by **revelation**, anchored in the character of a faithful God who cannot lie (Numbers 23:19).

At this level, the believer does not treat the Bible as a historical artifact or a religious reference. Instead, God's Word is received as a living revelation, a divine message actively working in the heart and life of the one who believes. Hebrews 4:12 confirms that the Word is living and powerful—not only instructing, but discerning, correcting, transforming, and creating. Faith at this dimension understands that Scripture is not static text—it is the expressed will and authority of God, carrying the same creative power that spoke the universe into existence (Hebrews 11:3).

When believers walk in this dimension of faith, they are no longer content with surviving life's storms or simply enduring hardship. Instead, they begin to **reign in life**, as promised in Romans 5:17: *"For if by one man's offence death reigned by one; much more they which receive abundance of grace and of the gift of righteousness shall reign in life by one, Jesus Christ."* This reigning is not circumstantial—it is positional, grounded in the finished work of Christ and accessed through unwavering faith. It is the believer's inheritance to walk in authority, speak with divine clarity, and manifest heaven's will on earth.

In this walk of reigning faith, the central question is no longer about God's ability or Christ's victory. Jesus has already won the battle at Calvary. The devil has already been disarmed (Colossians 2:15), and believers have already been given authority in His name (Luke 10:19). Therefore, the question is not, *"Will God come through?"* but rather, *"Will we believe Him enough to act on His Word?"* The responsibility now rests with us—to rise up in faith, to refuse to be swayed by what we see, and to live as those who take God at His Word.

This highest level of faith is a lifestyle marked by surrender, declaration, and dominion. It is not for the faint-hearted—it is for those who have determined that God's voice will be their compass, and His

Word their final authority. It is for those who are ready to move from merely quoting Scripture to embodying its power. This faith does not react to the world—it rules over it, not by force, but by standing firm on eternal truth. And in that position of unwavering belief, we find the secret not only to victory—but to walking in the fullness of our kingdom identity.

| 4 |

FAITH FOR THE SUPERNATURAL: ACCORDING TO YOUR FAITH

"What you receive from God will never rise above what you believe—faith is the doorway to the supernatural."

The Realm Beyond Logic-There comes a point in every believer's life when natural methods fail, human help fades, and logic no longer applies. It is in this moment that God invites us into the realm of the supernatural—the dimension where impossibilities bow to the Word of the Lord. This is not fiction. This is faith. And Jesus made the terms clear: "According to your faith, be it unto you." In this chapter, we explore what it means to live by a faith that transcends evidence, defies limitation, and invites the miraculous. The supernatural is not God's exception—it's His intention. And it's waiting, not for your perfection, but for your belief.

The journey of the believer is not merely intellectual; it is supernatural. To walk by faith is to live in alignment with the invisible realm of God's power, where natural limitations are overturned and divine possibilities become reality. In 1 Corinthians 2:4–5 (KJV), the Apostle Paul states, *"And my speech and my preaching was not with enticing words of man's wisdom, but in demonstration of the Spirit and of power: That your faith should not stand in the wisdom of men, but in the power of God."* This declaration draws a clear distinction between natural wisdom and spiritual demonstration, between faith based on information and faith rooted in divine revelation. Supernatural faith is what connects believers to the power of God, beyond the logic, limitations, and senses of the natural world.

Supernatural Faith According to God's Word

Supernatural faith is more than belief; it is a spiritual force imparted by God that allows us to trust in His promises even when every visible sign says otherwise. It is the kind of faith that holds firm when human reasoning fails, when physical senses are overwhelmed, and when natural solutions are exhausted. Hebrews 11:1 (KJV) defines faith as *"the substance of things hoped for, the evidence of things not seen."* Supernatural faith rests in the unseen reality of God's Word. It says, "I trust God with all"—my body, my future, my finances, my family, my assignment, and even my pain.

This kind of faith declares that God's Word is true even when nothing around me looks like it. Supernatural faith is not moved by what we see, hear, feel, taste, or touch—it is moved only by what God has said. This faith is rooted in complete surrender and unwavering dependence. It trusts God fully, not partially; confidently, not conditionally. And it is this kind of faith that gives heaven permission to invade earth and move on our behalf.

Natural Faith vs. Supernatural Faith: A Contrast of Foundations

Natural faith is grounded in what can be perceived through the senses and confirmed by external evidence. It relies on circumstantial assurance—on what appears reliable or predictable in the natural world. For example, a person exercises natural faith when they trust a bridge to hold their weight because they see its structure and know it has held others. However, this kind of faith is fragile under pressure; when circumstances shift or visual proof is no longer available, natural faith tends to unravel. It cannot survive in situations that require belief in the unseen, the unknown, or the supernatural.

Supernatural faith, by contrast, is rooted not in what we see but in covenantal authority—the unchanging, binding promises of God's Word. It is not based on outward conditions but on God's integrity, character, and faithfulness. Supernatural faith believes God's Word as final, even when circumstances scream the opposite. It is the kind of faith Abraham had when he believed God would make him the father of nations, though his body was as good as dead (Romans 4:18–21). Unlike natural faith, which collapses in the face of impossibility, supernatural faith is nourished in it. It flourishes under pressure, because pressure is the environment where God's power is most evident.

When the odds are stacked, when the diagnosis is terminal, when the account is empty, and when every visible sign says "no," supernatural faith confronts the crisis not with fear, but with the Word of God. It speaks what God has promised, expects manifestation, and refuses to be moved. While natural faith draws its strength from probability, supernatural faith draws from divine authority—and in doing so, it prevails where natural faith fails.

Faith: A Force That Changes the World

To trust God with everything is not just an act of devotion; it is a world-altering force. History has proven that men and women who walked in supernatural faith—Abraham, Moses, David, Esther, Elijah, Paul—turned the course of nations, split seas, raised the dead, conquered kingdoms, and overcame impossible odds. Hebrews 11, often called the "Faith Hall of Fame," recounts the stories of those who subdued kingdoms, stopped the mouths of lions, quenched fire, and gained victory—all by faith.

Supernatural faith is what causes the sick to be healed, the bound to be delivered, and the loss to be saved. It is what empowers ordinary people to do extraordinary things—not by human might, but by the Spirit of God working through believing hearts (Zechariah 4:6). This faith does not need backup plans—it relies solely on the One who cannot fail. It declares like Job, "Though He slay me, yet will I trust Him" (Job 13:15). It says like Mary, "Be it unto me according to thy word" (Luke 1:38). And it moves like Peter, stepping out of the boat at the mere sound of the Savior's voice (Matthew 14:29).

According to Your Faith—So Be It: Faith as the Doorway to the Supernatural

One of the most striking principles in the ministry of Jesus is captured in His words to two blind men in Matthew 9:29 (KJV): *"According to your faith be it unto you."* This profound statement reveals a key truth about the nature of God's power and our access to it—God responds to faith, not simply to need. The two men had a desperate situation, but it was not their condition that moved Jesus—it was their confidence in His ability to heal them. In other words, the measure of their faith became the measure of their miracle.

This truth turns our thinking upside down. Many people assume that because God is compassionate and omnipotent, He will automatically respond to crisis. But the biblical pattern is consistent: faith is the bridge between God's power and our experience. Jesus didn't say, "According to your pain," or "According to your need." He said, "According to your faith." That means our level of belief—our willingness to take God at His Word—determines what we receive from the supernatural realm. God's power is not withheld or limited; it is available and ready to flow—but it flows through the pipeline of believing faith.

This truth is repairing and challenging. It means that miracles are not reserved for a spiritual elite—they are available to "whosoever believes." Faith is the equalizer in the kingdom of God. The supernatural is not initiated by religious ritual or emotional desperation; it is activated by spiritual trust. As long as a person is waiting for things to make sense in the natural, they will remain limited to the natural. But once that person chooses to trust what God has said—regardless of what they see, feel, or fear—they step into the realm where all things become possible (Mark 9:23).

Supernatural faith is not reckless; it is radically obedient. It sees what others cannot, dares to believe when others doubt, and acts when others delay. It is the faith that builds arks before rain, steps into seas before they part, and speaks healing before symptoms change. It is not based on hype or hope—it is based on heaven's truth. When we embrace this kind of faith, we begin to experience the supernatural not as rare or random, but as a regular expectation of those who trust in a limitless God.

So now the question becomes deeply personal: Will you live by what you see—or will you live by what He has said? Will you allow circumstances to shape your belief, or will you let God's promises define your perspective? For those who choose to believe, the supernatural is not the exception—it becomes the new normal. Faith does not eliminate difficulty, but it guarantees divine intervention. It invites the miraculous into the everyday and reveals the power of a God who is ready to perform His Word in the life of anyone bold enough to believe it.

| 5 |

THE POWER OF BELIEVING: FAITH FOR LIFE'S CHALLENGES

"When sight fails, faith sees—believing is the vision that leads you through life's greatest battles."

The Vision of Faith-Sight is limited to what is seen. Faith sees what has not yet appeared and declares it as done. The power of believing is more than positive thinking—it is spiritual perception fueled by divine truth. In times of trouble, when the fog of fear tries to blur our vision, believing becomes the torch that lights our path. This chapter leads us into the mechanics of faith during crisis—when believing isn't easy, but it's essential. You'll learn how to develop spiritual eyesight, how to hold on to promises not yet fulfilled, and how to stand firm when natural sight fails. For the believer, faith isn't just a choice—it's the lens through which we must live.

Seeing Through Trials with Supernatural Vision

Life will always present moments of adversity, times when circumstances feel overwhelming, resources seem limited, and answers appear out of reach. But for the believer, challenges are not dead ends; they are divine invitations to exercise faith that transcends the natural. This kind of faith is not rooted in emotion, convenience, or sight—it is anchored in the unshakable truth of God’s Word. As trials press in, faith pushes back with confidence, declaring that what God has spoken outweighs what life presents. In the face of sickness, faith sees healing. In financial struggle, faith sees provision. In seasons of uncertainty, faith clings to the certainty of God’s promises. Faith for life’s challenges is not merely survival—it is victorious living that reflects the strength, peace, and endurance that comes from trusting a faithful God. It is sight beyond seeing—a vision that does not waver when the storm rises, but stands firm, knowing that the same God who brought you to it is more than able to bring you through it.

The Life of Joshua: Receiving by Faith Through Meditation and Focus

In Joshua 6:1–2 (KJV), Scripture records a pivotal moment in Israel’s history. Jericho, a fortified city with impenetrable walls, stood between the Israelites and the fulfillment of God's promise. Yet the Lord spoke with clarity to Joshua: *“See, I have given into thine hand Jericho, and the king thereof, and the mighty men of valour.”* Notice the tense—

God said, "I have given." The victory was declared before a single stone had fallen. God's Word always precedes manifestation. The promise existed in the spiritual realm, and it was through faith-filled obedience that Joshua and the people would bring it into the natural realm.

Rather than focusing on the height and strength of the wall, Joshua chose to focus on the Word of the Lord. He did not meditate on the problem—he meditated on the promise. This is a powerful principle of faith: what we meditate on will eventually dominate our thoughts, direct our decisions, and shape our destiny. Meditation is not merely repetition—it is a spiritual discipline that brings our mind and heart into alignment with the reality of what God has already spoken. According to Joshua 1:8 (KJV), God commanded Joshua, *"This book of the law shall not depart out of thy mouth; but thou shalt meditate therein day and night... for then thou shalt make thy way prosperous and then thou shalt have good success."*

Meditation on God's Word is what bridges the unseen to the seen. As we dwell on His promises, we begin to visualize them, to speak to them, and to receive them in our lives. Whether we are facing family crises, health challenges, or financial hardships, meditation opens our spirit to hear from the Holy Spirit, who will give us insight, wisdom, and strategic direction. As Jesus said, the Spirit will "guide you into all truth" (John 16:13), and in moments of pressure, He will show us the way forward. Meditation does more than bring comfort it births clarity and activates supernatural wisdom.

When Joshua faced Jericho, he wasn't given a military strategy in human terms. Instead, he received divine wisdom from above: *Walk around the city. Say nothing. Blow the trumpets. Shout.* It seemed foolish by natural standards, but it was God's ordained method. The key to Joshua's victory was not effort—it was obedient faith and spiritual focus. Through meditating on God's Word, he received God's plan, activated courage, and positioned Israel to step into the next chapter of their destiny. As it says in Joshua 1:6–7, God told him repeatedly, *"Be strong and of a good courage… be thou strong and very courageous."* Strength and courage are not manufactured through willpower; they are cultivated through fellowship with the Word of God.

The same principle holds true for us today. God's Word is our source of wisdom, direction, and victory. When we choose to meditate on it day and night, we train our minds to stay focused in a distracted world. Focus is not a luxury—it is a necessity. It is the gateway to all higher-level thinking: perception, memory, learning, problem-solving, and decision-making. Without focus, all aspects of our cognitive and spiritual life will suffer. Proverbs 16:20 (AMP) says, *"He who pays attention to the word [of God] will find good, and blessed (happy, prosperous, to be admired) is he who trusts [confidently] in the Lord."*

Likewise, in 1 Timothy 4:15–16 (AMP), Paul exhorts Timothy to *"Practice and work hard on these things; be absorbed in them [completely occupied in your ministry], so that your progress will be evident to all."* The Word must become our priority—not an afterthought. As we give ourselves wholly to the truth of Scripture, our advancement will be visible, undeniable, and unshakable.

| 6 |

Living the Life of Faith: From Revelation to Manifestation

"The just don't guess—they live by faith and watch the unseen take shape."

The Faith-Fueled Life-Faith is not a single act—it's a lifestyle. It is the rhythm of heaven that lived out in the soil of earth. From revelation to manifestation, every promise of God travels the road of faith. But faith is not static. It grows. It speaks. It moves. It endures. And most importantly, it manifests. This chapter will show you how to transition from hearing God's Word to seeing it fulfilled in your life. You'll explore how to sustain your faith in seasons of silence, how to align your confession with your convictions, and how to live in continual expectation of the supernatural. The God kind of faith doesn't visit occasionally—it abides permanently. And when it does, it changes everything.

Faith is not an isolated principle; it is the very rhythm of the believer's life. From the moment God speaks, we are invited to participate in a divine transaction: to believe what we do not see, to act on what we cannot control, and to trust what we cannot explain. As seen through every chapter, whether it be the **Law of Faith**, the **Battle of Faith**, **Faith for the Supernatural**, or **Faith for Life's Challenges**, one truth remains unshakable: **faith is the gateway to everything God has promised**.

From Abraham's obedience to Joshua's meditation, from the woman with the issue of blood to the centurion's bold command—each example affirms that **faith is not passive**. It is living, speaking, moving, and expecting. It transcends feelings and demands action. Faith takes God at His Word, especially when circumstances say otherwise.

In a world where distractions scream louder than truth and storms rise without warning, believers must not merely admire faith; they must **walk in it**. As we meditate on God's Word, declare His promises, and remain anchored in His presence, we tap into a power greater than reason, and a wisdom greater than the world. The God kind of faith does not beg for miracles—it **commands mountains to move**, knowing they must obey.

The God Kind of Faith: Living Beyond What You See

Are you ready to rise above life's limitations and live in the power of God's promises?

In *The God Kind of Faith*, Bishop C.H. Wright takes you on a transformative journey into the heart of biblical faith—not as a concept, but as a lifestyle. With deep scriptural insight, personal conviction, and Spirit-led revelation, this book will teach you how to move from mental agreement to mountain-moving belief.

From the battle-tested courage of Joshua to the healing faith of the woman with the issue of blood, every chapter equips you to hear God's voice, meditate on His Word, and walk in supernatural authority. Whether you're facing spiritual warfare, personal crisis, or simply hungry for more, this book will ignite your faith, sharpen your focus, and unlock God's best for your life.

You'll discover:

- The difference between natural and supernatural faith
- How to meditate on the Word until you see results
- How to fight and win the good fight of faith
- How to move from surviving to reigning through the Law of Faith
- Why bold obedience is the doorway to the miraculous

This isn't just another book on faith—it's a **call to live it**.

God has already given the promise. Now it's your time to believe, act, and receive—according to your faith.

Final Reflection

Don't meditate on the wall—meditate on the Word. The wall may be high, but God's promise is higher. The challenge may be great, but God's wisdom is greater. And the battle may be fierce, but the victory is already given. Focus your faith, renew your mind, and walk boldly in what God has already spoken—because the next chapter of your life depends on it.

APPENDIX

LIFE APPLICATION QUESTIONS

Use the following prompts for reflection, journaling, or group discussion:

1. **What promises of God are you struggling to believe today?** Are you allowing circumstances to drown out what God has already declared?

2. **Have you been meditating more on the problem than the promise?** What scriptures can you begin meditating on daily to strengthen your focus?

3. **Are you walking in natural faith or supernatural faith?** What would it look like to act on God's Word even before you see change?

4. **What spiritual walls must fall for you to move forward?** Have you asked the Holy Spirit for divine strategy?

5. **Are you ruling in life or just surviving?** What does it mean for you personally to reign in life by faith (Romans 5:17)?

Faith Declaration: Bold Confession for Believers

I believe God. I take Him at His Word. I walk by faith and not by sight. I declare that no wall is too high, no storm too fierce, and no challenge too great. I have been delivered from the power of darkness and transferred into the Kingdom of Light. I overcome by the blood of the Lamb and the word of my testimony.

I meditate on God's word day and night, and it guides every step I take. I operate in supernatural wisdom. I speak the Word with authority. I live by faith, fight by faith, and win by faith. My life is not led by fear, but by the voice of God. I will not shrink back. I will not compromise. I will walk in the fullness of my kingdom inheritance. According to my faith, be it. In Jesus' name.

Amen.

Final Charge: Walk Boldly—Faith Is the Key

You are not powerless. You are not forgotten. You are not waiting on God—**He is waiting on you** to believe, to act, and to rise.

This is your moment. You have been given the measure of faith. Now put it to work. Speak to the mountain. Declare the promise. Meditate on His Word. Obey without hesitation.

Let your life echo heaven's report: **"I have believed, therefore I have spoken"** (2 Corinthians 4:13). Walk boldly. Stand firmly. Believe relentlessly.

Because faith isn't just a concept, it's your kingdom lifestyle.

ACKNOWLEDGEMENTS

First and foremost, I give all honor and glory to my Lord and Savior Jesus Christ—the Author and Finisher of my faith. Without His grace, wisdom, and revelation, this book would not exist. Every insight and truth in these pages results from His divine guidance and unfailing presence in my life.

To my beloved family—thank you for your love, prayers, and unwavering support. You have stood by me through every chapter of this journey. Your encouragement has been the wind beneath my wings.

To my church family and ministry partners, your faith, dedication, and hunger for the Word have inspired me daily. You are a living testimony of the power of faith in action.

To the mentors, pastors, and spiritual leaders who have poured into my life, thank you for your obedience to God's call and your investment in my growth.

To every reader, preacher, and believer who longs to walk in the fullness of God's promises—this book was written with you in mind. May it ignite your faith and equip you to walk boldly in what heaven has already declared.

And finally, to the Holy Spirit—my constant companion, teacher, and guide—thank You for breathing life into every word, every chapter, and every message. May this work bear fruit that glorifies God and empowers His people.

— Bishop C.H. Wright

About The Author

Bishop Connie Wright is a native of Fayette County born in Moscow TN. He was united in holy matrimony to his high school sweetheart, Annie Wright and together, they are the natural parents of four and spiritual parents of many.

He founded House of Faith Ministries in May 1987 with seven members attending services. This year he and HOFM celebrated 36 years of faithful leadership. In addition to the Somerville location, he has established HOFM campuses in Bolivar and Alamo TN. In May 2022, the doors of The Venue, House of Faith's banquet hall and event center, were opened. The Venue is located in the heart of Somerville in the building formerly known as Fred's.

A carpenter by trade, Bishop Wright has been building and renovating churches and homes since the 80's. He has been instrumental in renovations at House of Faith's campuses and he and his wife are real estate investors.

Under his leadership, House of Faith has been active in the community over the years. They have renovated homes, provided temporary housing for displaced women and children, supported the efforts of nonprofits in the community and much more. He is a father, husband, pastor, and prolific leader. He has authored two books, *The Power of Choice*, and *The God of Increase.*

Made in the USA
Columbia, SC
21 June 2025

59706354R00052